MBS

CBS

NBC

NBC

12 GREAT MOMENTS THAT CHANGED
RADIO HISTORY

by Angie Smibert

12 STORY LIBRARY

www.12StoryLibrary.com

12-Story Library is an imprint of Peterson Publishing Company and Press Room Editions.

Produced for 12-Story Library by Red Line Editorial

Photographs ©: AP Images, cover, 1, 6, 11, 12, 14, 17, 20, 21, 29; Library of Congress, 4; Shutterstock Images, 5; Bain News Service/Library of Congress, 7, 9; Underwood & Underwood/Library of Congress, 8; Bettmann/Corbis, 10, 13, 16, 18, 19, 22, 28; Russell Lee/Library of Congress, 15; Michael Ochs Archives/Corbis, 23; Douglas Kent Hall/Corbis, 24; Amy Sancetta/AP Images, 26; Stockbyte/Thinkstock, 27

ISBN
978-1-63235-026-8 (hardcover)
978-1-63235-086-2 (paperback)
978-1-62143-067-4 (hosted ebook)

Library of Congress Control Number: 2014946804

Printed in the United States of America
Mankato, MN
October, 2014

Go beyond the book. Get free, up-to-date content on this topic at 12StoryLibrary.com.

TABLE OF CONTENTS

1

THE FIRST RADIO MESSAGE CROSSES THE ATLANTIC

On December 12, 1901, three short clicks traveled across the Atlantic Ocean on radio waves. The clicks represented dots in Morse Code. They spelled the letter S. They were being sent from a 200-foot (61 m) tall transmitter. The transmitter was in a place called Poldhu, Cornwall, on the English coast. The message was received more than 2,000 miles (3,218 km) away by a 400-foot (122 m) tall antenna in St. John's, Newfoundland, Canada. This S was the first transatlantic radio message. The man responsible for this message was Italian inventor Guglielmo Marconi.

Guglielmo Marconi with his radio equipment

9,104

Length, in miles, of telegraph cable that connected San Francisco, California, to Manila, the Philippines, via Midway Island and Guam in 1903.

- A message was sent from a transmitter on the coast of England and received in Canada.
- The clicks in the message represented the letter *S* in Morse Code.
- The man responsible was Italian inventor Guglielmo Marconi.

The signal from Poldhu was received at Signal Hill, St. John's, Newfoundland.

Five years earlier, a 22-year-old Marconi had demonstrated and patented his wireless receiver in England. He had read about experiments with radio waves. He saw the possibilities for using them to carry messages. Radio waves are a form of electromagnetic radiation. This radiation is a kind of energy that travels in waves through space. These waves can be smaller than an atom or bigger than the earth. Radio waves have the longest wavelengths.

In 1897, Marconi started the Wireless Telegraph and Signal Company. Two years later, he sent his first message. It traveled from shore to a ship 20 miles (32 km) away. Over the next 15 years, his company built permanent wireless stations around the world. They were used mainly to communicate with ships at sea. Marconi won the Nobel Prize in Physics in 1909 for wireless telegraphy.

RADIO TELEGRAPHY SAVES LIVES

"Come at once. We struck an iceberg. Sinking." Jack Phillips tapped out this message in Morse Code at 12:17 a.m. on April 15, 1912. Phillips was one of two wireless telegraph operators aboard the RMS *Titanic*. For the next two hours, the *Titanic*'s radio room exchanged a flurry of messages with other vessels nearby. The *Titanic* sent its last message at approximately 2:25 a.m. At approximately 4 a.m., the RMS *Carpathia* arrived. It rescued more than 700 people from the icy waters of the North Atlantic. Jack Phillips was not among the survivors.

The *Titanic* was a British passenger ship on its first trip to New York

The *Titanic* departs from Southampton, England, on April 10, 1912.

City. The vessel was the largest ship afloat at the time. It carried 2,224 passengers and crew on this voyage. The *Titanic* was equipped with a Marconi wireless. This radio telegraph had a range of 250 nautical miles (460 km).

Fifteen minutes before the *Titanic* hit the iceberg, the ship's wireless operators were busy. Messages were coming in from a Canadian wireless station. At the same time, another ship was trying to warn the *Titanic* of icebergs. These messages jammed the signals aboard the *Titanic*. Jamming may have also contributed to the confusion after *Titanic* hit the iceberg. The radios on nearby ships had trouble sorting out the messages. The United States passed the Radio Act of 1912 because of the *Titanic* disaster. It required all ships to maintain 24-hour radio watch. They had to keep in contact with nearby ships and coastal radio stations.

705

Estimated number of people saved from the *Titanic*.

- The *Titanic* struck an iceberg shortly after midnight on April 15, 1912.
- The distress signal was sent by a wireless radio operator.
- The disaster led to changes in the laws governing ships and radios.

RADIO SPREADS SPORTING EVENTS NEWS

"Hooray for Dempsey!" one listener cried at the radio. Thirty seconds earlier, boxer Jack Dempsey had knocked out Billy Miske. They were in the third round of the heavyweight championship bout in Benton Harbor, Michigan. Francis Edwards of the *Detroit News* Radiophone Service read the results of the fight on the air. It was Labor Day afternoon in 1920. Station WWJ in Detroit had just brought the first sporting event to radio.

The broadcast was not live. The announcer got the results over the telephone and read them on the radio. The *Detroit News* was

Boxer Jack Dempsey training in 1922

one of the first newspapers to install a radio station. It covered approximately 100 miles (160 km). The signal reached 300 radios owned by amateur operators. These operators could send and receive radio signals. People would gather at an operator's house or business to listen to music. Now, they could listen to sports scores and other news. Sports fans usually had to wait a day to find out scores in the newspapers. A month after the boxing match, WWJ brought listeners more news. It broadcast the scores of the 1920 World Series. Soon, many stations were reporting on all kinds of sports. Eventually, radio began broadcasting live sporting events. Boxing matches, baseball games, and football games were all popular live events.

634
Number of dedicated sports radio stations in the United States in 2010.

- The first sporting event announced on the radio was a boxing match in 1920.
- Approximately 300 radios were tuned in.
- The *Detroit News* relayed the results over WWJ radio in Detroit, Michigan.

New York City Mayor John Hylan throws out the first pitch at the 1920 World Series.

4

COMMERCIAL RADIO BEGINS REGULAR PROGRAMMING

On November 2, 1920, the words "This is KDKA" opened the first commercial radio broadcast. KDKA was a radio station in Pittsburgh, Pennsylvania. That day, the announcer read the results of the presidential election. He reported Warren Harding had become president.

The KDKA broadcast out of a tiny shack in East Pittsburgh. The shack was atop one of Westinghouse Electric's buildings. The company was one of the leading makers of radios. Westinghouse thought a radio station with regular programming would help sell more radios. Engineer and amateur radio enthusiast Frank Conrad set up the station. Conrad already played records for friends over his own experimental

KDKA broadcasters at work on the night of the 1920 presidential election

Baseball stars Babe Ruth (left) and Dazzy Vance (right) speak with NBC radio sportscaster Graham McNamee.

WHERE DID THE NETWORKS COME FROM?

Many of today's major TV networks started out as radio networks. In the 1920s, companies owned multiple radio stations. They saw an advantage to linking them together and broadcasting programs over a network of stations. NBC (National Broadcasting Company) was formed in 1926. CBS (Columbia Broadcasting System) began broadcasting in 1929.

station, 8-X-K. KDKA was the first station to offer daily programming. It broadcast sports scores and political news. It also shared church services, weather forecasts, and information on crops and the stock market. KDKA became a popular way for people in the Pittsburgh area to receive news. Soon hundreds of other commercial stations cropped up across the country.

1,000
Estimated number of people listening to KDKA's first broadcast.

- KDKA in Pittsburgh was the first commercial radio station in the United States.
- "This is KDKA" were the first words broadcast by the station.
- The announcer gave the results of the 1920 presidential election.
- Soon, hundreds of commercial stations appeared across the nation.

ADVERTISING CHANGES HOW RADIO IS FUNDED

"Leave the congested city and enjoy what nature intended you to enjoy!" The first radio ad begged listeners to escape Manhattan, a heavily populated part of New York City. It urged them to come see beautiful new apartments in Queens, a suburb. WEAF in New York City played this 10-minute commercial on August 28, 1922. The ad was the first in a series.

Soon other advertisers, such as the credit card company American Express, were buying airtime for commercials. Other companies sponsored entire radio programs. These businesses wanted to be

Gracie Allen (center) and George Burns (right) before a taping of *Burns & Allen*

THE GOLDEN AGE OF RADIO

The 1930s was considered the Golden Age of Radio. During the Great Depression, people turned to their radios for news. But they also enjoyed dramas, comedies, musical and variety shows, soap operas, and game shows. These shows helped them take their minds off hard times. Some of the most popular programs were the *Lone Ranger* and *Burns & Allen*.

associated with popular programs. They paid a fee to sponsor the show. Most radio shows were named after their sponsors. The *Lucky Strike Radio Show* and the *Chase and Sanborn Hour* are just two examples.

Advertisers invented new kinds of shows to reach people who might buy their products. Soap operas, for instance, were designed to sell cleaning products to women. Advertising continued to influence what shows played on the radio—until television came along. When

$100
Cost of the first radio commercial on WEAF.

- The ad ran in New York City.
- Other businesses soon began running commercials.
- Many companies sponsored whole programs.

advertisers flocked to the new medium, they took their shows with them.

The stars of the *Chase and Sanborn Hour* David Rubinoff (left), Eddie Cantor (center), and James Wallington (right)

FDR USES RADIO TO CALM A NATION

On a Saturday night in 1933, Americans heard a reassuring voice on the radio. "My friends, I want to talk for a few minutes with the people of the United States about banking." It was the voice of newly elected President Franklin Roosevelt. He was speaking to a scared nation.

The country was in the middle of the worst economic

President Roosevelt addresses the nation in a fireside chat on October 14, 1938.

Roosevelt spoke to Americans in a direct and personal way.

period in history. It was called the Great Depression. A quarter of the American people were out of work. The banks had just failed. Over the radio, President Roosevelt explained what happened to the banks. He explained how he was going to handle the problem. He ended with the words, "together we cannot fail." Roosevelt spoke to Americans as if they were in the room with him.

This was the first of Roosevelt's 28 radio talks. President Roosevelt called them his fireside chats. Roosevelt spoke directly to the people throughout the Depression and most of World War II (1939–1945).

13:42

The amount of time the first fireside chat lasted on March 12, 1933.

- The president used the radio to talk the American people.
- The country was in the middle of the Great Depression.
- Roosevelt explained the banking crisis.
- He calmed the fears of the nation.

THINK ABOUT IT

Today, presidents talk to the public on TV and online. Ask an adult to help you find a video of a recent presidential address online. Compare it with the description of FDR's fireside chats on these pages. Which one would you rather listen to or watch? Use evidence from the video and these pages to support your answer.

15

RADIO BRINGS DISASTER INTO OUR LIVING ROOMS

The *Hindenburg* flies over New York City on May 1, 1936, nearly a year before it burst into flames.

The *Hindenburg* was ready to land. It floated over its mooring station at Lakehurst, New Jersey, on the evening of May 6, 1937. The airship was a long, rigid, blimp-like aircraft. These aircraft were also called dirigibles. The *Hindenburg* was nearly as large and grand as the RMS *Titanic*. It used a highly flammable gas to stay afloat. It had already made 10 successful trips from Germany to the United States. At 7:21 p.m. the dirigible dropped its landing lines. The ground crew began guiding it in.

Herb Morrison from WLS in Chicago was on the ground. He was recording a radio report on the *Hindenburg*'s arrival. Suddenly, smoke and flames sprang from a section of the dirigible and spread rapidly. "It's burning, bursting into flames and is falling on the mooring mast and all the folks, we—" Morrison reported. He was emotional as he described what was happening. "This is one of the worst catastrophes in the world! ...Oh, the humanity..." The *Hindenburg* was destroyed in 34 seconds. Thirty-six people died that day.

3

Number of hours Morrison recorded on the *Hindenburg* disaster.

- Radio reporter Herb Morrison recorded the *Hindenburg* disaster.
- The report played on national radio stations and changed the way news was reported on the radio.

Morrison recorded his emotional eye-witness account of the disaster. The next day, he was interviewed live on NBC radio. During the interview, NBC played parts of Morrison's recording. The interview aired on radio stations across the country. It was the first time NBC ever aired a news report nationally. The *Hindenburg* disaster spelled the end of dirigible travel. However, it marked the beginning of reporting on events as they happened.

The scene of the *Hindenburg* disaster

THE WAR OF THE WORLDS PANICS AMERICA

On the evening on October 30, 1938, the voice of an announcer broke into a radio music program. He reported on strange explosions happening on the planet Mars. The music resumed. A few minutes later, the announcer broke in again. He interviewed an astronomer about the explosions. This interview was soon interrupted by a report of something crashing to Earth near Grovers Mill, New Jersey.

Orson Welles rehearses *The War of the Worlds.*

Most listeners knew this was a radio drama. Some people, though, thought America was under attack by Martians. In Newark, New Jersey, for instance, a whole block of people rushed out of their houses. They had wet cloths over their mouths. They believed they were running away from a Martian gas attack. The next day, the *New York Times* reported "a wave of mass hysteria seized thousands between 8:15 and 9:30 o'clock last night."

Welles met with reporters after *The War of the Worlds* caused a panic.

These panicked people should have turned in right at 8 p.m. They would have heard, "The Columbia Broadcasting System . . . presents Orson Welles and the Mercury Theater of the Air in *The War of the Worlds* by H. G. Wells." The Mercury Theater was a regular Sunday evening program on the CBS radio network. Orson Welles and his cast dramatized many different stories. Wells' novel, *The War of the Worlds*, is about a Martian invasion in the early 1900s. Orson Welles adapted the story. It sounded like a live newscast of an invasion happening in New Jersey. The next morning, the newspapers called for an investigation. Welles apologized for causing panic. However, *The War of Worlds* made the Mercury Theater of the Air famous.

62
Number of minutes in *The War of the Worlds* broadcast.

- The radio play *The War of the Worlds* was broadcast the day before Halloween in 1938.
- The story was based on H. G. Wells' novel *The War of the Worlds*.
- Orson Welles and the Mercury Theater of the Air presented the radio drama.
- Some people panicked because they thought Martians were really invading Earth.

EDWARD R. MURROW BRINGS WORLD WAR II HOME

"This is Trafalgar Square," the voice on the radio calmly announced. Listeners could hear air raid sirens wailing in the background. The voice described searchlights catching the clouds in the night sky. It described footsteps walking the dark streets of London as "ghosts shod with steel shoes."

The voice was CBS reporter Edward R. Murrow. It was August 24, 1940. World War II was under way. The Germans were warming up to bomb London heavily in what was called the London Blitz. Murrow and other US reporters had been in England and Germany covering the war since

Murrow on the streets of London in 1940

8

Number of months the London Blitz lasted.

- American reporter Edward R. Murrow broadcast live radio reports during the London Blitz.
- The reports were called *London After Dark.*
- Murrow described London and its people as the city was being bombed by the Germans.

it started in 1939. On this day in 1940, Murrow started a series of live reports called *London After Dark.*

People slept in the subways to avoid bombs during the London Blitz.

He painted a vivid picture of life in war-torn London. He even broadcast from the rooftops of buildings during some of the worst of the bombing. He began most broadcasts with the words "*This* is London." And he ended them with what many Londoners told each other every night: "Good night, and good luck." Murrow brought the war to American listeners across the Atlantic Ocean from London.

THINK ABOUT IT

Radio, TV, and the Internet have the ability to impact how people feel about war. Imagine you were hearing Murrow's broadcast in 1940. How would hearing his coverage of the bombings change how you feel about the war? Would you want to help the British or allow them to face the Germans alone? Why?

ROCK AND ROLL FINDS A HOME ON THE RADIO

A disc jockey's gravelly voice called out, "The old Moondog Rock and Roll Party is under way…on WJW Cleveland!" The old Moondog's name was Alan Freed. Freed started playing rhythm and blues records on his overnight show in the spring of 1951. Freed coined the term *rock and roll* for the mixture of rhythm and blues and popular music he played. The name stuck.

DJ Alan Freed was the first to popularize rock and roll on the radio.

Freed's shows attracted rock and roll stars such as Bo Diddley (in red jacket).

On March 21, 1952, Freed promoted and hosted a dance at the Cleveland Arena. It was called the Moondog Coronation Ball. The dance featured some of the best rock-and-roll bands from the area. This show is considered the first rock concert.

The first hour of the show went relatively smoothly. However, more than 20,000 people showed up without tickets. They tried to get into the show. A riot broke out. The dance had to be canceled.

The next evening, Freed explained on air what happened. He asked his audience to let the radio station know if they supported him. By the end of the show, phone calls and telegrams flooded the station. Later, letters of support came in the mail.

Everyone wanted the Moondog to stay. Instead of being canceled, Freed's show was made an hour longer. Rock and roll on the radio was here to stay.

$1.75
Price of a ticket at the door to the Moondog Coronation Ball in 1952.

- Cleveland disc jockey Alan Freed started playing a mixture of rhythm and blues and pop music on the air.
- He coined the term *rock and roll* for this mixture of music.
- The show—and rock and roll—became a hit on the radio.

FM RADIO PLAYS ALBUM ROCK

On April 7, 1967, disc jockey Tom "Big Daddy" Donahue walked into the KMPX radio station. He carried bags full of his favorite record albums. The studio was in an old warehouse by the docks in San Francisco, California.

An experienced AM radio DJ, Donahue wanted to play longer songs by rock bands such as the Doors, the Rolling Stones, and

The Rolling Stones were one band that produced albums with songs longer than those played on AM radio.

43

Percentage of homes in the United States with FM radio in 1967.

- DJ Tom Donahue played longer songs by rock bands.
- Donahue's show was very popular.
- Other stations started playing album rock, too.
- Album rock helped make FM more popular.

AM VERSUS FM

Though not popular until the 1970s, FM radio was invented in 1935 by Edwin Armstrong. FM had better sound quality and range. However, AM radio was already well established. FM radio required new equipment such as transmitters and receivers. For that reason, owners of AM stations and radio manufacturers discouraged the development of FM radio.

Bob Dylan. These artists were releasing long-playing records, also known as albums. Some songs were up to 14 minutes long. AM radio stations cut these songs down to as little as two minutes. Donahue went on the air at 8 p.m. He played the kind of music AM stations would not play. Within 10 days, his show was very popular with listeners. By August, KMPX played rock music 24 hours a day.

KMPX was one of many FM stations playing album rock in the late 1960s and early 1970s. The album rock format did not last beyond the late 1970s. But by then, FM had

become the radio most Americans listened to. In 1967, the Federal Communications Commission ruled radio stations in larger cities had to put more original programming on their FM stations. This created thousands of hours of airtime that needed to be filled. Some stations played classical music on FM. Some played jazz. Many others discovered rock.

SATELLITES MAKE RADIO AVAILABLE ANYWHERE

On September 25, 2001, radio left the earth. That was the day the first satellite radio company, XM, began broadcasting. Its competitor, Sirius, started four months later. This new kind of radio service did not use AM or FM radio transmissions. Instead, it transmitted music and programming from a satellite. The radio signal went directly to digital receivers in cars, homes, and portable devices.

Satellite radio listeners can drive across the country listening to the same station. There are no advertisers on satellite radio. Instead, listeners buy subscriptions. In 2008 the two satellite radio companies merged into SiriusXM. By 2014 SiriusXM

Listeners can tune into the same satellite radio station nearly anywhere in the United States.

had 26.3 million subscribers. That year, vehicles made by 42 car manufacturers worldwide came with satellite radio.

99
Percentage of the United States, in square miles, covered by satellite radio.

- The first satellite radio provider, XM, launched in 2001.
- Satellite radio is broadcast from a satellite in orbit above the earth.
- The service is paid for by subscribers instead of advertisers.
- People can listen to radio stations on the Internet, too.

Many people now listen to the radio online.

Another new way to listen to the radio is through the Internet. Online radio started with Internet Talk Radio in 1993. It was a program about computers. The next year, the Rolling Stones played the first concert over the Internet. WXYC in Chapel Hill, North Carolina, became the first traditional radio station to broadcast online. Today most radio stations stream their programming online. Others exist only online.

FACT SHEET

- Heinrich Hertz discovered radio waves and demonstrated them in 1888. Other scientists built on this discovery with their own inventions. This led to the development of radio. However, there is some controversy about who actually invented radio.

- Italian inventor Guglielmo Marconi used radio waves to send messages in Morse Code. He patented his wireless telegraph in Britain in 1896. He proved radio could be used over long distances. Wireless telegraphy became the primary way ships communicated for the next decade or so.

- Other inventors contributed to radio in its early days. American Reginald Fessenden was the first to transmit voices over the radio in 1903. He used a method that changed the height of the radio wave to carry the sound. This was the beginning of AM radio. In 1933, Edwin Armstrong invented another way for radio waves to carry sound. He changed the speed at which the radio wave travels. This was the beginning of FM radio.

- In 1947 William Shockley of Bell Laboratories invented the transistor. It is a small device that conducts electricity. The transistor replaced the bulky vacuum tubes in radios and other electronic devices. Radios could then be much smaller and cheaper.

- Today people can listen to the radio without an AM or FM signal. Satellite radio allows listeners to tune into the same station no matter where they are in the country. Internet radio streams radio programs online.

GLOSSARY

AM
A system for sending radio signals where the height of a radio wave is changed so information can be sent in the form of sound.

astronomer
Person who studies the stars, planets, and other objects in space.

broadcast
Sent over television or radio.

electromagnetic radiation
Energy waves caused by the interaction between charged microscopic particles.

FM
A system for sending radio signals where the number of radio waves per second is changed so information can be sent in the form of sound.

Morse Code
A system of sending messages using long and short sounds, flashes of light, or marks to represent letters and numbers.

satellite
A machine that is launched into space and orbits around the earth.

telegraph
A system of sending messages over long distances by using electrical signals.

transmission
Passing of radio waves between two radio stations.

wavelengths
Distances from one wave of energy to another as the waves travel.

FOR MORE INFORMATION

Books

Garner, Joe. *We Interrupt This Broadcast: The Events That Stopped Our Lives—from the Hindenburg Explosion to the Virginia Tech Shooting.* Naperville, IL: Sourcebooks MediaFusion, 2008. Print.

Goldsmith, Mike. *Guglielmo Marconi.* Austin, TX: Raintree Steck-Vaughn, 2002. Print.

McCarthy, Meghan. *Aliens Are Coming!: The True Account Of The 1938 War of the Worlds Radio Broadcast.* New York: Knopf, 2006. Print.

Websites

FCC's History of Radio
www.transition.fcc.gov/cgb/kidszone/history_radio.html

FCC's How Radio Works
www.transition.fcc.gov/cgb/kidszone/faqs_radio.html

The War of the Worlds: Live at the Fitzgerald Theater
www.radiolab.org/story/91622-war-of-the-worlds

INDEX

About the Author

Angie Smibert is the author of several young adult science fiction novels, numerous short stories, and a few educational titles. She also worked at NASA's Kennedy Space Center for many, many years. She received NASA's prestigious Silver Snoopy as well as several other awards.

32